Glen Alpine Springs Hotel

A History of Burke County's
Finest Accommodation

Louisa Emmons

Glen Alpine Springs Hotel: A History of Burke County's Finest Accommodation

Hollow Tree Press
P.O. Box 322
Morganton, NC 28680

All inquiries should be addressed to the author through the publisher.

Printed in the United States of America

❧❧❧

About the Author

Louisa Emmons is the great-great granddaughter of Colonel Thomas George Walton who built Glen Alpine Springs Hotel shortly after the Civil War. Emmons is also the author of *Tales from a Civil War Plantation: Creekside*, which is the story of the plantation built by Colonel Walton in 1836. The book won the Robert Bruce Cooke Family History Book Award from the North Carolina Society of Historians in 2014. Another book by Emmons, *Civil War Voices from Western North Carolina: Letters from the Battlefield and the Home Front* won the Society's Willie Parker Peace History Book Award in 2015.

Dedication

This book is dedicated to the faculty and students of the
Glen Alpine Springs School (1902-1909).

Acknowledgments

I would like to thank the following individuals who assisted me in making this book possible: Laurie Johnston, Curator of the North Carolina Room, Morganton Public Library, for assisting me in my research; Picture Burke for permitting the reproduction of a number of historic photographs in this book; and my mother, Mary Boggs Alexander, who shared family stories about Glen Alpine Springs Hotel with me.

Preface

When I set out to write about Glen Alpine Springs Hotel, I had some reservations (no pun intended). I felt that such a grand and imposing work of architecture deserved to have its story told, and I felt something of an obligation to my family to be the one to tell the story. Truthfully, however, little remains of that grand hotel---two hotel registers, several room keys, a billing form, a number of newspaper articles, a few old letters, some family stories and a lot of lore about what I like to call the "glory days" of Glen Alpine Springs Hotel. It amazes me that such a splendid structure which operated for over twenty years could have so entirely disappeared from history. Nevertheless, I have collected the remnants that I could find, and I have put them together to try and recreate something like a shadow of that grand hotel. I like to imagine Glen Alpine Springs Hotel as it must have been at one time with its grand ballroom lit by chandeliers, with couples dancing to the music of an orchestra, with the sound of laughter and sparkling voices borne on the air… What a tale those voices would tell us if they could!

Louisa Emmons
December 2015

A Brief History of Mineral Springs Resorts in Western North Carolina

Hot Springs

Native Americans first discovered the healing springs in Madison County which would later become known as Warm Springs and, finally, Hot Springs. Artifacts discovered at the springs verify that the Cherokee believed in the healing powers of the springs long before their discovery by white settlers. The Natural Hot Mineral Springs, as they were called in 1778, were rediscovered by white mountain settlers eager to experience the healing waters whose temperatures exceeded 100 degrees. A tavern was established by the springs in 1788. It became a popular stopping place during the American Revolution, serving drovers who guided their livestock along the trail that ran between Greenville, Tennessee and Greenville, South Carolina. The tavern was a notorious location for murder and robbery.

The building of the Buncombe Turnpike in 1828 greatly increased the number of people interested in "taking the waters" of the mineral springs in Madison County. The turnpike was a toll road that ran from Asheville to Warm Springs and into Tennessee. James Patton, and his brother John, bought the springs in 1831 and built the 350 room Warm Springs Hotel also known as Patton's White House. The dining room seated 600 guests. Colonel James Rumbough purchased the Warm Springs Hotel in 1862, enlarging it in 1882. When the hotel burned in 1884, Rumbough did not have the money to rebuild and the land was sold to the Southern Improvement Company. The company built a new resort called the Mountain Park Hotel. When nearby springs of a higher temperature were discovered in 1886, the Southern Improvement Company changed the name of the town from Warm Springs to Hot Springs.

Mountain Park Hotel

Mountain Park Hotel was an elegant and popular resort hotel, one of the most fashionable in the country. It consisted of a 200 room hotel, stables, a bath house with sixteen marble pools, a spring house, croquet and tennis courts. The elegant hotel reflected a Swiss style of architecture with a fashionable mansard roof. The guest rooms were lighted with electricity and heated by steam. The golf course was the first organized club in the southeastern United States. The interest in Mountain Park Hotel and its healing waters waned in the early 1900s, and in 1917 the hotel and grounds were leased to the federal government. The once-elegant resort was used as an internment camp for German sailors and civilians captured in American harbors at the onset of World War I. Mountain Park Hotel burned in 1920 and was never rebuilt, though two lesser hotels were built on the site over the next forty years, both eventually being destroyed by fire.

Sulphur Springs

Sulphur Springs in Asheville, North Carolina, was discovered by Robert Henry and his slave Sam in 1827. Once a spiritual retreat for the Cherokee, Henry's son-in-law, Reuben Deaver, built a wooden hotel on a hill above the springs in 1830. Within ten years, Deaver's hotel had 500 summer guests. Most visitors were low-country South Carolina planters, among them the Pinckneys, Pickens and Alstons. The Alstons reserved a second floor room from May to September every year. Deaver's hotel featured a large ballroom with a string band of free African American musicians, cabins, bowling alleys, billiard tables, and shuffleboards. The hotel burned down in 1862 but was rebuilt in brick in 1887 by developer and philanthropist Edwin G. Carrier of Philadelphia and named Carrier Springs. It later operated under the name The Hotel Belmont and was operated by Dr. Karl Von Ruck of Ohio. The hotel had the first electric elevators in the South. Between 1889 to 1894, an electric railroad shuttled tourists from Asheville to the hotel. Although the hotel burned in 1891, it remained a popular spot for picnicking and horse-drawn carriage rides for many years.

Postcards of The Hotel Belmont on Haywood Road in Asheville

The Old Spring House at Sulphur Springs

Eagles Nest Hotel

White Sulphur Springs Hotel

Eagles Nest Hotel
and White Sulphur Springs Hotel

Though the Eagles Nest Hotel and White Sulphur Springs Hotel were both located in Waynesville, North Carolina, they occupied unique geographical locations.

The Eagles Nest Hotel perched atop Mount Junaluska and commanded the surrounding countryside at a breathtaking elevation of 5,000 feet. The Eagles Nest Hotel could house 80 guests. Twelve visitors at a time took a three-hour stagecoach ride of five miles up the mountain to the summit of Mount Junaluska to reach the Eagles Nest. In April 1918, the Eagles Nest Hotel was destroyed by fire.

White Sulphur Springs Hotel, prized for its mineral waters, could accommodate 200 guests and was situated near the middle of the town of Waynesville. In April 1918, White Sulphur Springs Hotel was purchased by the United States military as a sanitarium for soldiers recovering from respiratory ailments resulting from World War I. The Spring House (pictured right) is all that remains of the resort. A stone monument in front of the Spring House memorializes the once-popular vacation spot.

The Cabins at Thompson's Springs

Healing Springs Hotel

Thompson's Springs

William Barker discovered the presence of healing springs in Ashe County, North Carolina, in 1883 while helping his father plow. William "Willie" Barker went to get water for his father from a nearby stream and discovered a hidden spring which came to be called Healing Springs. According to accounts verified by his father, the water brought to him by young Willie cured both of them of poison oak within twenty-four hours. Willie's sister was said to have been healed of tuberculosis by the same mineral waters, though her tubercular twin sister had succumbed before the discovery of the spring.

Captain H.V. Thompson from Virginia acquired the springs in 1887 with the hope of developing them into a popular resort. Thompson built a hotel at the site of the springs in 1888 and changed the name to Thompson's Springs. The property included a restaurant, a hotel with community rooms and guest rooms. The hotel accommodated 75 guests and was open from May to November. In 1889, a gazebo was built over the spring and it's healing waters were bottled and sold. *Thompson's Bromine-Arsenic Water* was in great demand; within a ten year period from 1889 to 1899, fifty wagonloads per day of water were shipped out to customers. The response was so overwhelming eight cabins were built to contain the overflow of guests eager to try the waters at Thompson's Springs.

In August 1962, the hotel at Thompson's Springs was destroyed by a fire so intense the two story structure was burned to ash in sixty minutes. The cabins were not damaged and remain intact today. The spring was untouched.

4

Connelly Springs Hotel

Connelly Mineral Springs

William Lewis Connelly, an officer in the North Carolina militia, was the first known settler in Connelly Springs, North Carolina. As a former captain in the North Carolina Militia, he had participated in the relocation of the Cherokee in the "Trail of Tears" for which service he was promoted to colonel. Upon completion of his military service, he and his wife Elizabeth Moore Connelly built a log cabin and took in boarders who traveled on the stagecoach line which ran between Salisbury and Asheville. He also provided fresh horses for the stagecoach. In time, a settlement grew up around his cabin, and a post office was built. The community was called "Happy Home."

In 1885, property owned by Elmira Connelly was found to have healing mineral springs which she made available to those who were interested in the restorative powers attributed to the waters. People arrived by horse, wagon and train to take away five-gallon containers of the healing waters which contained large amounts of bicarbonate of iron.

The Connelly Mineral Springs Hotel was constructed in 1886 along the railroad track near the springs. The hotel was built by Thomas and Philip Maroney of Salisbury, and featured fifty guest rooms, a large dining room and a ballroom. The hotel was dismantled in 1944, and the town was incorporated as Connelly Springs in 1920.

The Spring House at Connelly Springs Hotel

Walton And Pearson, Proprietors

Thomas George Walton

Thomas George Walton was born in Morganton in 1815, the grandson of William Walton of Amherst, Virginia, who journeyed to Burke County in the late 1700s as one of the Overmountain Men. Walton's father, of the same name, became a prominent merchant and civic leader in Burke County.

T. G. Walton was named president of the Board of Directors of the Morganton Branch of the Bank of North Carolina in 1859. In 1871, he served as vice-president of the North Carolina Agricultural Society. He was appointed state agent of salt distribution for Burke County by Governor Zebulon Vance and was an active promoter for the building of the Western North Carolina Railroad. He would later serve as one of its directors in 1873. Walton was a member of the State Legislature and a director of the State Asylum in Raleigh (later known as Dorothea Dix Hospital) in 1897. From 1875-1877, he was an organizing director and later Secretary-Treasurer of the Western North Carolina Insane Asylum in Morganton, later called the State Hospital in 1890.

Walton was commissioned as a Captain at the outbreak of the Civil War in 1861 but resigned his commission upon the reorganization of his company and then served as Colonel of the 8th Regiment of North Carolina Home Guards from 1862 until the end of the war.

A member of Grace Episcopal Church in Morganton, Colonel Walton served as a vestryman for fifty years and as a lay reader. Instrumental in founding Grace Episcopal Church and helping to select its first minister, Colonel Walton was devoted to church and family. In 1858, T.G. Walton became Senior Warden and served in that capacity until his death in 1905.

Married to Eliza Murphy in 1836, T.G. Walton built a plantation home in Morganton at the age of twenty-one which he named "Creekside" because of its close proximity to Silver Creek. He and his bride lived in a one-room building adjacent to Creekside while the house was being built. This structure, which sat atop a Revolutionary War era foundation would later become incorporated into the design of the house as the back wing of Creekside.

In 1865, when Stoneman's Raiders swept through western North Carolina, Union General Alvan Gillem and his men took Creekside as their headquarters. Though the house was ransacked, furniture was burned and destroyed, and food stores were raided and depleted, the house was spared the fate of being burned.

After the Civil War, Colonel Walton fostered and financially supported children from Burke County who had been orphaned by the war.

Above is a photograph of the Walton family in the early 1900s. Colonel T.G. Walton is shown seated in the front center (circled). John Pearson appears at the left of the photograph (circled) with his wife, Florence Walton Pearson to his right. At the front right side of the photo is Herbert H. Walton (circled) whose vivid description of Glen Alpine Springs Hotel remains the only detailed account of an eyewitness to the glory days of the resort. The setting for the photo is the Walton family home, Creekside, pictured below.

John Pearson

John Pearson was born in Morganton in 1852, the son of Robert Pearson and Jane Tate, members of two old Morganton families. He was thirteen years old when Stoneman's Raiders rode through Morganton at the end of the Civil War.

The Western Railroad began construction in 1855, and its tracks came to within six miles of Morganton by the outbreak of the Civil War. By the last year of the war, the tracks extended to Camp Vance in Burke County, and they reached Morganton in 1868. Governor Tod Caldwell, a native of Morganton, appointed 16-year-old John Pearson to be a conductor on the Western Railroad on the route from Salisbury to Morganton. Pearson served in that position for four years by which time the tracks had been completed all the way to Old Fort in McDowell County. Thereafter, Pearson was affectionately called "Captain Pearson," a title rightfully earned because of his service on the railroad.

When Pearson left service on the railroad, he went into business with L.A. Bristol of Morganton. From that time, he participated in many business ventures including banking, operating a brick-making firm, a sash and blinds manufacturer, a Grace Hospital trustee, and the operator of a cash warehouse which paid local farmers cash for their produce. John Pearson operated a feed, grain and coal business known as *John H. Pearson & Co.* for over 50 years on Sterling Street and then Greene Street in Morganton.

Pearson served as mayor of Morganton and served in the State Legislature. He was appointed to the Railroad Commission in 1898. In 1920, Pearson served as a delegate to the Democratic National Convention in San Francisco and was a passionate supporter of women's suffrage.

As a lifelong member of Grace Episcopal Church in Morganton, John Pearson was a delegate to the convention that formed the Episcopal Diocese of Western North Carolina.

He served as Senior Warden at Grace Episcopal Church from 1915 to 1942 at which time he resigned, although the church refused to accept his resignation. Pearson also served as a vestryman for over 60 years.

John Pearson married Florence Walton, a daughter of Colonel Thomas George Walton in 1878, and they had eight children. In 1890, he built a large brick Victorian home on West Union Street in Morganton. The property was sold to the First Baptist Church in the 1950s, and the Pearson house was torn down to make room for the construction of a new church.

John Pearson died at the age of 101, having often expressed a desire to live to be 100 years old. Residents of Morganton referred to him as the "Grand Old Man" in recognition of his jaunty step, the flourish of his cane, and the manner in which he doffed his hat on the street when he encountered friends.

John H. Pearson is shown above, seated with his family in the entrance of his family home located at 502 West Union Street in Morganton. Pearson's wife, Florence Walton Pearson, is shown standing at his left. The Pearson home and property, below, was sold in the 1950s and demolished to build the First Baptist Church.

The McEntire Inn and the Walton House Hotel

The Walton family had a history of managing inns and hotels prior to the construction of Glen Alpine Springs Hotel. Colonel Walton's father, Thomas, had married Martha McEntire, the daughter of successful businessman James McEntire of Rutherfordton. The McEntire Inn of Morganton, built by James McEntire, faced the courthouse on the southwest corner of South Sterling and West Union Streets. First known as the McEntire Inn, it was operated by William McEntire. After the death of William McEntire, the inn became known as the Walton Hotel and was operated by Thomas George Walton's sons, James Thomas Walton and Edward "Stanley" Walton. Advertising for the Walton Hotel read: "Clean Beds, Comfortable Rooms, Polite and Attentive Servants, a Fine Bar, and a Free Omnibus." By 1874, the Walton Hotel, with its stagecoach office, was Morganton's largest hotel. By the late 1800s, the Walton Hotel was rented by

railroad contractor Atwood Hunt, and it became the Hunt House. It was destroyed by fire in 1893 together with a number of other buildings in downtown Morganton.

The McEntire Inn of Morganton, above, would become the Walton Hotel and then the Hunt House before being destroyed by fire in 1893.

Glen Alpine Springs Hotel: The Glory Days

"*In* a mountain nook, quiet and secluded even in the busy twentieth century rush, lie a few piles of rock, part of a fallen chimney and an old stone wall--all that remains of the once gay and popular Glen Alpine Springs Hotel. The mineral springs were first discovered by Colonel Moulton Avery, father of the late I.T. Avery, and he found the mountain cove at once so cool and delightful and beautiful a spot that he erected a cottage and spent many happy weeks there with his family."

"After the turmoil and devastation of the Civil War, Colonel T.G. Walton, dreamed of a gathering place in which people would be cheered, benefited in health and gain a new and cheerful view of their lives still shattered by the disheartening result of the war. Such a dream grew in magnitude until it came into being from an English architect's pencil---one Charles Collier. The building was erected with an expenditure of thirty thousand dollars ($30,000). Begun in 1876, it was completed in 1877. It contained fifty rooms all comfortably and tastefully furnished. One entered an immense lobby which by night grew into the ballroom, where the gay and lighthearted ladies and gallants danced the Lancers and Virginia Reel, interspersed with occasional waltzes. This room was lighted with four large kerosene chandeliers, each containing four lamps. As the evening grew in gaiety, the gentlemen walked downstairs to the bar below where could be bought the finest of wines, French brandies and all manner of liquor. The parlor was the "room of many windows." It stood in the tower and was plastered white with walnut trim in the English fashion. The dining room contained two large chandeliers and smaller lights on either side of each and every window. This room measured

40 x 50 feet and here elegant meals were served with much of the food...being sent from New York."

"A promenade on top of the roof ran the entire length of the hotel and on fine nights the Negro orchestra repaired to it and the dances were held under moonlight and starlight in the very shadow of the mountains against which the hotel nestled. For amusement, the guests had a billiard and pool room, a ten pin alley and croquet was enjoyed on the huge lawn, which swept under towering oaks and spruces almost out of sight. A homemade flying jenny likewise graced this lawn with seats instead of horses. The rooms in the hotel were spacious and comfortable, and the wide front piazza delightful to rest on and view the beautiful surrounding country. The stairway was unusual in that the banister rails were alternating maple and walnut."

"The hotel boasted three springs---the Temple one, a lovely affair with a huge soapstone bowl, had lythia and alum minerals, one down a steep ferny incline was sulphur, and still further was a cool delicious, tasteless pool perhaps containing a little iron, but known as the "Free-Stone Spring."

"There were eight cabins for the exclusive mortals who preferred to be far from the noise of the dance and the smell of frying chicken. Some of these were built by private individuals, one being Neilson Falls, the first (grandfather of Buck Falls). He and his wife resided there every summer. Some cabins had two rooms and some just one. Three mountains rose directly behind and to the sides of the hotel---Monte Crucis was so named because a giant spruce which was in the exact shape of a cross grew on its summit, Propst Knob, the highest peak in the South Mountains and Cyst Gap."

"A hack drawn by four horses met the train at Glen Alpine Station (name changed from Turkey Tail to that of the hotel by Col. Walton) daily. This was nine miles from the hotel and quite a journey in those days. The train brought guests from as far east as Wilmington and as far west as Old Fort. Those coming from Asheville had to come by stage coach to Old Fort."

"Glen Alpine Springs operated as a hotel until 1900, was later sold and used as a mountain school, then abandoned until it nearly rotted down, then burned up about six years later, it is said, from a bootleg still."

These are the words of Louise Walton Boggs, the granddaughter of Colonel T.G. Walton, who wrote what her father, Herbert H. Walton, related to her years later about the glorious days of Glen Alpine Springs Hotel.

The hotel was built by Colonel Thomas George Walton, and financially supported by his son-in-law, John H. Pearson, both of Morganton, North Carolina, in a section of Burke County called Brindletown. It was Colonel Walton's intention that its guests find relaxation, healthful revitalization, and an escape from the harsh memories of the recent Civil War.

According to the hotel register, Glen Alpine Springs Hotel opened for business on July 17, 1878 and operated during the summer months. Daily rates were $2.00, weekly rates were $8.00 to $10.00 according to the location of one's room, and monthly rates were $20.00 to $25.00. Children and servants stayed for half-price and horses were stabled.

Billed as the largest frame structure in the state, the hotel was larger than the state capitol. It contained 50 rooms within its three story framework. The wood-paneled dining hall seated 200 guests. None of the bedrooms was smaller than 20 feet by 24 feet with 18 foot ceilings. The grand ballroom was lit by four huge kerosene chandeliers, each containing four lamps. Visitors arriving by train disembarked at the community known as "Turkey Tail" whose name changed to Glen Alpine Station, and from there, guests were taken by horse and carriage for the eight mile journey to the hotel.

The five mineral springs which provided the healing waters sought by guests included alum, blue sulphur, magnesium, iron and lithium.

Dinners were lavish with offerings of such items as venison, mutton, local beef, trout and wild turkey. Some food items were shipped from New York.

Most of the guests who came to Glen Alpine Springs Hotel were members of the wealthy social strata, many of them of the planter class. The luxurious appointments of the hotel provided the kind of elegance to which they were accustomed: music, dancing, hunting, fishing, gold digging, billiards, bowling and croquet.

Notable guests who stayed at Glen Alpine Springs Hotel included B.S. Gaither, A.C. Avery, Benjamin Duke, Samuel McDowell Tate, R.V. Michaux, J.C. Mills, L.A. Bristol, C.F. McKesson, Jay Gould, Dr. W.A Collett, W.H. Vanderbilt, Governor Zebulon Vance and John Perkins. The names of other guests at the Glen Alpine Springs Hotel include entries from surrounding states and as far away as New Orleans, Baltimore, New York and London.

GLEN ALPINE SPRINGS,

A. A. BANKS, PROPRIETOR.

This popular resort will be open for visitors June 1, 1892.

Visitors should leave train at Morganton, N. C., for the Springs, stopping at the Hunt House, and they can obtain any kind of conveyance they wish to take them on to the Springs.
The proprietor will do all in his power to make his guests happy and contented.
Band of music and amusements of various kinds will enliven the season.
The house will be first class in every department. Satisfaction guaranteed. Address,   A. A. BANKS, Prop'r.
may26 tf.   Morganton, N. C.

Though an advertisement whose date is not discernable lists A.A. Banks as a proprietor for Glen Alpine Springs Hotel, no record of his tenure as proprietor can be found in the hotel register.

Glen Alpine Depot

The History of "Turkey Tail"

"At Glen Alpine, five miles west of Morganton, the railroad reaches an elevation of 1,315 feet, the highest railroad point in Burke County. The little town...had its beginning after the Southern Railroad was built through that section about 1868. Sometime after 1876, J.D. Pitts set up a planing mill near the railroad station, and about the same time two brothers, Columbus and Edward Sigmun, started a country store there, and took charge of the little country post office. The name of the place was then changed from Turkey Tail to Sigmundsburg. A few years later the Glen Alpine Springs Hotel was built about eight miles south of the station. For a number of years...this boosted the passenger service of the railroad. The passengers were conveyed to and from the hotel by hacks. In 1883, the little town which had grown up around the railroad station was incorporated as Glen Alpine."

From *Sketches*, by Cordelia Camp.
The News Herald, March 27, 1964

Management Changes

Although Glen Alpine Springs Hotel began under the proprietorship of Thomas G. Walton and John H. Pearson, a number of changes in management came during the twenty some years in which the hotel was in operation. These changes become clear when documents from the time of the hotel are examined.

Prior to 1880, pamphlets and advertisements list Walton and Pearson as the proprietors of the hotel. In 1880, an advertisement for the hotel lists Adolphus J. Rutjes as proprietor. The same advertisement also indicates a change in policy from earlier days when the hotel operated only during the summer. The advertisement states that the hotel is now open "Summer and Winter."

Interestingly, Adolphus J. Rutjes, originally from New York, is listed as a defendant in a Burke County court case "Bailey v. Rutjes and Others" outlined in the *Charlotte Home and Democrat*, April 1882, in which two of the defendants, Walton and Pearson, are questioned as to whether they entered into a contract to secure lumber for building and repairs on Glen Alpine Springs Hotel. Both Walton and Pearson insist that no contract exists between them and the plaintiff since Rutjes had "leased the premises for five years" and was responsible for any debts incurred during that time period.

The names of proprietors of the Glen Alpine Springs Hotel were maintained in the hotel register. The following is a list of proprietors with the date when they assumed management noted in the register. Examining the dates, it becomes apparent that the five-year lease of Adolphus Rutjes was never fulfilled:

Walton and Pearson	July 1877
Adolphus J. Rutjes	March 1879
C.S. Smith	August 13, 1880
Jenkins & Knott	April 28, 1880
John Pearson	April 18, 1882
Solomon Pool	July 1, 1884

W.H. Morrison	April 29, 1894
Walton and Walton	June 11, 1896
Walton and Bro.	July 15, 1896
C.S. Smith	June 1, 1897
Mr. J.T. Walton	July 3, 1897

Several things should be noted about the management changes at the hotel. First of all, the astonishing number of proprietors who managed the Glen Alpine Springs Hotel raises some questions about the stability of the hotel as a business venture. It is common knowledge among the descendants of Colonel Walton that he spoke despairingly about suspected dishonest business dealings that were associated with the hotel during his lifetime. These questionable business practices probably drained significant profits from the hotel. In addition, the Colonel stated during his lifetime that the large number of family members who enjoyed the privileges of Glen Alpine Springs Hotel without paying for them created financial problems. One only needs to examine the hotel register to note the large number of Waltons, Pearsons and various cousins who were regular patrons of the hotel. It is a tribute to the unfailing generosity and hospitality of Colonel Walton that he welcomed them with no apparent expectation of reimbursement.

With regard to the proprietors, a number of them were family members. Walton and Pearson, of course, were related by marriage. C.S. Smith was Charles Stuart Smith, a son-in-law who was married to Colonel Walton's daughter Martha Matilda Walton. Interestingly, a son of Charles Stuart Smith and Martha Matilda Walton Smith was born at Glen Alpine Springs Hotel while they were visiting in 1884. His name was William Walton Smith. In the entries which list "Walton and Walton" and "Walton and Bro.," it should be remembered that two of Colonel Walton's sons, James Thomas Walton and Edward "Stanley" Walton were experienced in the hotel business; one or both of these entries surely refers to them. The last proprietor listed undoubtedly refers to James Thomas Walton.

The Blue Ridge Blade
Sept. 14, 1878

Glen Alpine
Adv. (with picture)

Glen Alpine Springs, Burke County, North Carolina.

Eight miles from Station of same name on WNCRR will be opened for the reception of visitors on Wednesday the 17th of July. The road to the springs is an exceptionally good one, level and well shaded. Coaches meet all trains.

These Springs are situated immediately in the South Mountains, distant one and a half miles from Propst's Knob, one of the
UNITED STATES SIGNAL STATIONS.

The first story being 17 feet between floors, well lighted and ventilated, and having spacious verandas. A Roof (Mansard) Promenade of 115 feet, affords the finest mountain view from any
INHABITED SPOT IN NORTH CAROLINA!

Following closely the plans of our English architect we have a building presenting a fine architectural appearance and affording first class
ACCOMMODATIONS FOR TWO HUNDRED GUESTS
BILLIARDS, CROQUET, TEN PINS!

GOOD MUSIC THROUGHOUT THE SEASON.

Rates of Board: $30 per month, $10.00 per week, $2 per day. Liberal reductions for families.

For further particulars address,
WALTON & PEARSON
MORGANTON, NORTH CAROLINA

The Morganton Star
May 29, 1885

THE CELEBRATED GLEN ALPINE SPRINGS.

The following unsolicited letter just received, proves beyond a doubt that the celebrity which Glen Alpine Springs has acquired for its wonderful curative properties is well deserved:

LUCAMA, WILSON COUNTY, N.C.,
May 16, 1885.

Mr. T.G. Walton, Morganton:

Dear Sir:--What will be the cost of filling five 5 gallon demi-johns and shipping to me of the mineral water from the Glen Alpine Springs, freight excepted?

I visited these valuable springs in 1874 and again in 1876 and received more benefit from the waters than anything that I have ever taken in the way of medicine. The first visit I stayed at the springs three months and gained in weight 26 pounds, never having weighed more than 100 pounds up to that time, and when I left I weighed 125 pounds. I have some kidney trouble now, and think if I had some of the water, I would be benefitted by it. My business is such at this time that I cannot visit the springs, as I would like to do, but if I go to any watering place this summer, I shall be sure to go where I received so much benefit before--Glen Alpine. Hoping you will write me what the cost will be for the above quantity of water delivered at your depot.

Yours very truly,
L.F. LUCAS.

The Morganton Star
Aug. 27, 1886

SUNRISE NEAR GLEN ALPINE SPRINGS.

(Correspondence of The Star)

On Saturday morning, the 21st of August, 1886, I went to the summit of Raven's Cliff, near Glen Alpine Springs. The air was fresh, crisp, and balmy. It was freighted with the fragrance of rich, rare flowers, and the wood-notes wild of mountain birds, when I reached the summit the stars had just withdrawn their shining. Then came the dappled dawn. The hills were fog-crowned and the valleys mist-robed. In the crest glowing East are streaks of gray and gold. Now Apollo, full robed in spangled sheen, comes from his couch of fire. The drops of crystal dew gleam like oriental pearls. The rich foliage of the trees, touched with a shimmering light, glows like wings of gold. The mists and fogs roll away, and in their stead, high up in blue ether, cherubim and seraphim, pillowed in fleecy drapery, float with the balancing clouds. Now what a rapturous vision rolls up before mine eyes. On my right were great blue encircling mountains, whose splintered crags and fluted columns stand the silent sentinels of ages. On my left were great tall forests undulating the breezes of a golden summer, suggestive of the solemn majesty of God. In my front were great sweeps of fertile valley, intersected by silvery streams and reeking with the exhalations of the morn. I involuntarily pulled off my hat in that August presence and exclaimed with reverence, "In wisdom Thou hast made them all."
C.M.

The Morganton Star
Sept. 10, 1886

GLEN ALPINE SPRINGS.

(Correspondent of the Star)

BURKE COUNTY, N.C. Sept. 8.--The healing waters of this beautiful health, and pleasure resort, combined with the numerous natural attractions, have given this hotel a fair proportion of patronage this season. Guests who have been here annually since Col. Walton opened the house declare that it's almost like another home to them, and Rev. Dr. Sutton, of Raleigh, told the writer that two weeks spent here restored whatever vigor he had lost and built him up for another year's work. Last evening some of the guests of the house enacted a charade for the amusement of their fellows: This little comedy was cast as follows:

Matrimony, 1 act, 4 scenes. Dramatis personae: Count Lorenzo de Veurich, foreign nobleman, alias John Brown the barber, Mr. John Haige, of Fayetteville. Charles Harper, Mrs. Hamilton's nephew. Mr. C.F. McKesson, of Glen Alpine Springs, Dennis, a blundering Irishman, Mr. John C. Allen, of Canton, Ohio. Mrs. Hamilton, a rich widow(?), Miss Hattie Kincaid, of Athens, Ga. Arabella and Ellen, the widow's daughters, Miss Vollers, of Wilmington, N.C. Kate, lady's maid, Mrs. F. H. Barr, of Morganton.

A stage improvised from the dining room tables served every purpose. The acting was spirited and unusually good for amateurs. Everybody fell in love with the charming widow Hamilton (Miss Kincaid) who off the stage is a lovely and prepossessing blonde, and with her graceful daughter Ellen (Miss Vollers) and they laughed until their sides ached at the comicalities of the pseudo count.

Excellent vocal and instrumental music was rendered by Prof. Baker, of Charlotte, and his wife. The entire audience joined in singing, to the tune of "Little Brown Jug", a series of doggerel verses, lined out to them, with this chorus---

"Ha, Ha, Ha, you and me,
Glen Alpine Springs, how we love thee."

Dr. A.L. Leighthill, of Boston, is here with his accomplished wife. The doctor has started up the Carolina Queen mine and expects to begin ore-crushing either Saturday or Monday. Some seventeen veins have been laid bare by a series of cross cuts, and such samples of ore as have been taken from them are quite rich in gold. If when all the ore has been worked the results are one-half what they promise to be then there will be a big boom for this mining district.

JOEL.

An advertisement for Glen Alpine Springs Hotel in *The Blue Ridge Blade*, September 14, 1878 (top).

Correspondence to T.G. Walton from L.F. Lucas published in *The Morganton Star*, May 29, 1885 (above left).

Articles about Glen Alpine Springs Hotel published in *The Morganton Star* on August 27, 1886 (center right) and September 10, 1886 (bottom).

GLEN ALPINE SPRINGS,
NEAR MORGANTON.
BURKE COUNTY, WESTERN NORTH CAROLINA.

OPEN SUMMER AND WINTER.

WALTON & PEARSON,
PROPRIETORS.

GLEN ALPINE SPRINGS,
BURKE COUNTY, WESTERN NORTH CAROLINA.

These waters have proven of inestimable value and efficacy in a wide range of diseases, viz: in pulmonary and scrofulous affections, dyspepsia, bladder and kidney derangements, uterine and other disorders peculiar to females.

In confirmation of this statement, we refer all interested to the following persons:

Hon. Victor C. Barringer, Cairo, Egypt.
Rev. T. P. Johnson, Charlotte, N. C., late missionary to Turkey.
George Setzer, Esq., Catawba Station, W. N. C. R. R.
Dr. A. Powell, Catawba Station, W. N. C. R. R.
Mrs. Mary Propst, Glen Alpine, N. C.
Alfred Scott, Esq., Morganton, N. C.
Henry Sprague, Esq., " "

There are five mineral springs.

RATES

Board, per day,	. . . . .	$2 00
" " week,	. . . . .	10 50
" " two weeks,	. . . .	20 00
" " month, 28 days,	. . .	35 00

Special arrangements with families and for the season. Children and servants half price.

For further particulars, address

WALTON & PEARSON, PROPRIETORS,
Morganton, Burke Co., N. C.

April, 1879.

A pamphlet advertising Glen Alpine Springs in April 1879:
"The hotel is new, and is the largest frame building in the State, with the finest and best ventilated and furnished rooms in the South, the first story being seventeen feet between floors. Spacious verandas surround the building. A roof promenade of 115 feet affords the finest mountain view from any inhabited spot in North Carolina. The architecture of the building is a beautiful combination of Gothic and modern, and is much admired. The hotel affords first class accommodations for two hundred guests."

Raleigh, N.C.
April 17, 1879

Mess. Walton & Pearson
Glen Alpine Springs
Morganton, N.C.

Dear Sirs

We will print and bind 500 copies pamphlet for Springs, with covers, 8 pages small pica type for $15.00__1,000 copies for $20.00.

These prices are for first class job. We hope to have your order,

Yours Very Truly,
Edwards Broughton

We send samples of work of this style. Will you not need letter heads and envelopes, cards, circulars etc. Shall be pleased to give you low prices and good work.

E. Broughton

The document on the left, above, is a blank billing form of the type used at Glen Alpine Springs Hotel. When completed, it would have listed the expenses incurred during a stay at the hotel. At the time when this form was used, Adolphus Rutjes was the proprietor at the hotel.

The document on the right is a letter which was written on the reverse side of the billing form. It appears to be from former proprietors, Jenkins & Knott, to T.G. Walton and John H. Pearson. It reads:

Glen Alpine, N.C.

Sept 6, 18—

Mess. Walton and Pearson,

Gents, you will please come in this week, we wish to have settlement. We are going to leave here Monday or Tuesday next week, the 12th or 13th of this month.

Respectfully,

Jenkins & Knott

J.H. Pearson, Esq.

Dear Sir

There are matters pertaining to the post office that require your immediate attention.

Respect,

B.H. Knott

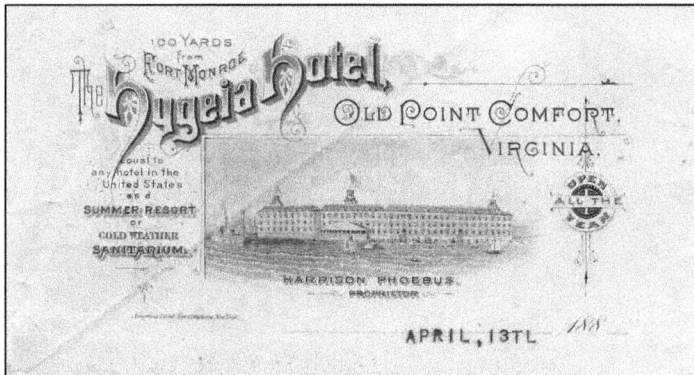

April 13th 188-

Mess. Walton & Peterson [Pearson]
Morganton, N.C.,

Gentlemen:

S.M. Shoemaker, Esq., of Baltimore has written me concerning a water that you are the agents of. If your water has merit, I will do anything I can to assist you in bringing it before the public. There have been, for the past two months, several hundred of the best people of this country, here, and they are generally of a class who have some physical ailment, and if they could be started in, or humbugged into drinking the water which, in my opinion, has got to be used in the same way that Moses used the serpent in the wilderness, "so must they have faith in the water to be lifted up…The fact is I have been there. I think I have drunk 17 barrels of water, for troubles in connection with the bladder and kidneys, and I am fully persuaded it is a delusion and a snare. I will not say this to the public, however, other people, whose judgment is better than mine settle these matters. I shall be glad to hear from you, and will do anything I can to help you introduce the water.

Yours respf'y,
H. Phoebus

D. C. PEARSON, POSTMASTER. L. A. BRISTOL, ASST. P. M. FRED TURNER, CLERK.

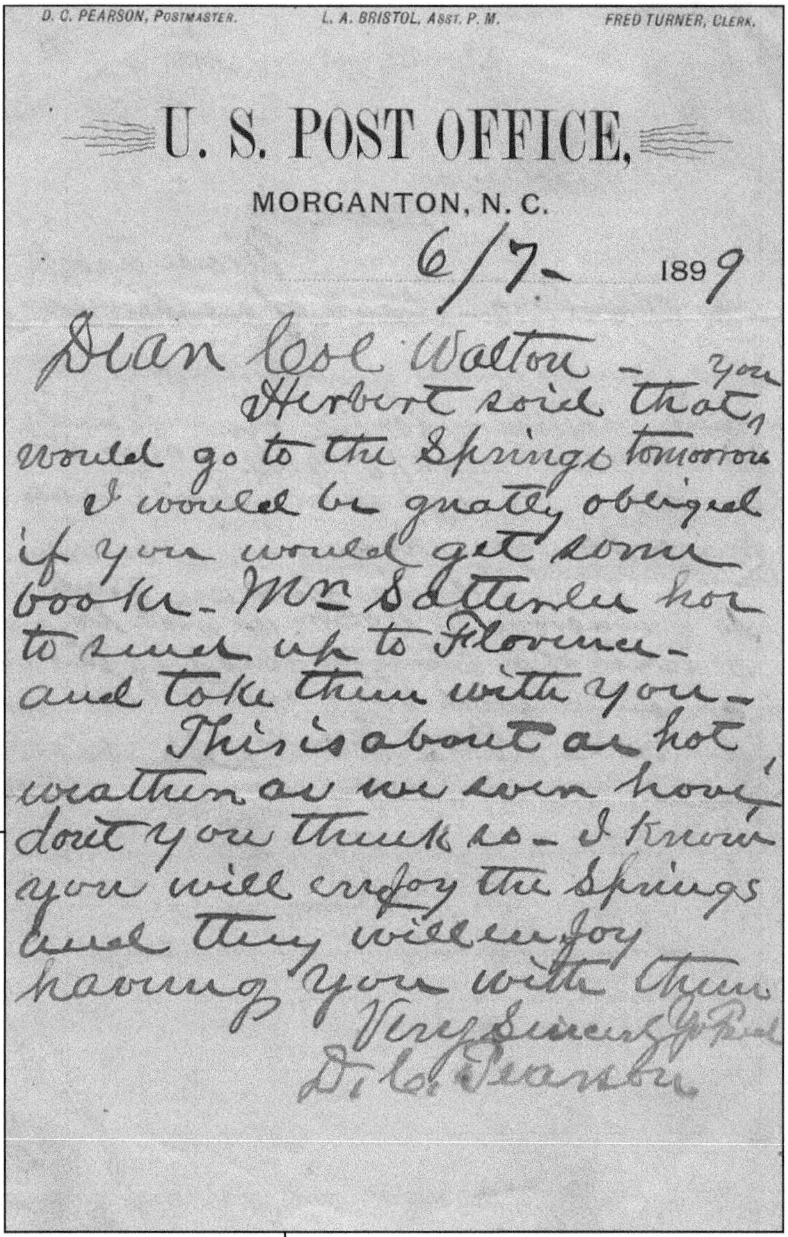

U. S. POST OFFICE,

MORGANTON, N. C.

6/7- 1899

Dear Col Walton - you
Herbert said that,
would go to the Springs tomorrow
I would be greatly obliged
if you would get some
books - Mr Satterlee has
to send up to Florence -
and take them with you -
This is about as hot
weather as we ever have,
dont you think so - I know
you will enjoy the Springs
and they will enjoy
having you with them
Very Sincerely Yr friend
D. C. Pearson

6/7 1889

Dear Col Walton,

Herbert said that you would go to the Springs tomorrow. I would be greatly obliged if you would get some books Mr. Satterlee has to send up to Florence, and take these with you. This is about as hot weather as we ever have don't you think so. I know you will enjoy the Springs and they will enjoy having you with them.

Very Sincerely,
D.C. Pearson

Morganton, N.C.
April 27, 1898

T. Geo Walton

Dear Sir,

Your request that I write you the effect that the Glen Alpine water had on me when I was suffering with some kidney trouble has been received. Before I visited the Springs I could hardly get my kidneys to act at all without taking medicine to make them. After spending a few days there I was entirely relieved from the trouble, and have never had a recurrence of it. That was in the Summer of 1896.

S.R. Collett

I regard it the best water I have ever seen for the kidneys.

GLEN ALPINE SPRINGS HOTEL,
BURKE COUNTY, N. C.

WALTON & PEARSON,
Proprietors,

August 17th

DATE	NAMES	RESIDENCE	ROOM

Sunday August 17

W. H. Moare, N. C.
J. Pearson — N C — 2 S
Dr R C Pearson — Morganton N. C. 2 S
Error W. J. Woodward Africa — 27 P

Monday August 18th 1879

Hon Z. B. Vance — N C — D
Hon T. Gettation Crekside 37 8
Hon J. A. Soooker Oxford Engl

Tuesday August 19th

J. Gettattle — Ashville N C 37 L
Jno C. Arthur — Columbia S C 37 L
Geo. Grew & Wife — Wilson 12 L

Wednesday Aug 20

The register at Glen Alpine Springs Hotel indicates that North Carolina Governor Zebulon Vance (above) was a guest at the hotel on Monday, August 18, 1879. Another entry lists Governor Vance's son, Zeb Vance, Jr. (below) as a guest at the hotel on August 22, 1878.

Thursday August 22nd

Z. B Vance Jr N O S N A D
Noah Bris & Lorb Scotland

22

On Tuesday, July 18, 1882, William Henry Vanderbilt, son of Cornelius Vanderbilt, and Jay Gould stayed at Glen Alpine Springs Hotel. Both William Henry Vanderbilt and Jay Gould were prominent New York railroad magnates and philanthropists.

Sale of Glen Alpine Springs Hotel and Lands.

As Commissioners appointed by a decree of the Superior Court of Burke county in a special Proceeding for partition therein pending entitled "T. George Walton, et al, ex parte," we will on

Monday the 21 day of May, 1900,

[the same being the day of sale designated in said decree], expose to sale for cash to the highest bidder at the court house door in the town of Morganton, all those certain tracts of land known as the Glen Alpine Springs Hotel property described and bounded as follows:

1st Tract. Beginning on a large, poplar, now down, known as McDaniel's corner in a hollow on the south side of a small branch, and runs N. 100 poles to a sycamore in the fork of the creek; thence E. 160 poles to a stake; then S. 100 poles crossing the creek to a stake on the side of mountain; then W. 160 poles to the beginning.

2nd Tract. Beginning on a white oak on the line of the first tract and runs W. 20 poles to a stake; then S. 140 poles to a stake; then E. 160 poles to a stake; then N. 40 poles to the beginning; also second tract purchased from B. S. Gaither, beginning on a stake N.-W. of the Sulphur springs and runs N. 22 poles to a stake in a marked line; then E. 110 poles to a pine on a ridge; then S. crossing the big cliff road and creek to a chestnut on the S. side of Monte Crucis just below a ditch; then S. 70 W. 72 poles to a stake; then W. 20 poles to a pine; then N. 46 W. 48 poles to the corner of the 50 acre tract on the bank of the creek; thence with the "Glen Alpine 100 acre tract to the beginning, containing 75½ acres more or less; also a piece or parcel of land beginning on the sycamore corner and runs N. 36 degrees W. 26 poles down the creek to a rock in the Ezell line; then E. 12 poles to a stake then S. 22 poles to the beginning including the Sulphur Springs.

Sale for partition among the tenants in common.

This 21st day of April, A. D. 1900.

W. S. PEARSON,
W. C. ERVIN,
Commissioners.

The key to Room 3 from
Glen Alpine Springs Hotel

The exact date when Glen Alpine Springs Hotel closed its doors is unclear, but a newspaper article announcing the sale of the hotel and lands appeared in a Burke County newspaper on April 21, 1900, one month before the date of the scheduled sale.

Glen Alpine Springs School

The founding of Glen Alpine Springs School began with an idea from Mrs. Isaac T. Avery of Morganton who was an owner of the former Glen Alpine Springs Hotel property. Mrs. Avery envisioned opening a mountain school in the former hotel. She enlisted the aid of a Mrs. Grant, a wealthy widow who had moved to Valdese from New Jersey in 1900. Mrs. Grant had the financial means to assist in the project, and she returned to New Jersey seeking a suitable person to operate the school. A family member of Mrs. Grant's deceased husband introduced her to a cousin, the Reverend Mr. R. Dalzell Schoonmaker, At the

time, Schoonmaker, a Presbyterian minister, was interested in identifying a worthy project to occupy his time and fulfil his calling. A graduate of Princeton University and Princeton Seminary, Reverend Schoonmaker had recently cancelled plans to perform missionary work in Africa due to illness. The founding and operating of a mountain school seemed the answer to his yearning to serve.

Converting the hotel into a mountain school began in the spring of 1902 with renovations and repairs being undertaken by Reverend Schoonmaker, Frank Boyd, and Hiram Herman of Hickory. According to *The News Herald* of April 19, 1963, "The hotel dining room was changed into a large assembly room and classroom. Two bedrooms became a dining room; two others were turned into kitchens. Still another became a utility room. Water…was piped from a branch in the mountains into the kitchen. Other bedrooms [became] carpenter rooms, classrooms, etc."

According to the same newspaper article, "the rooms to the right of the entrance on the first floor served as a lunch room, those to the left as classrooms. Girl students were quartered on the second floor right and the male students on the second floor left. Directly to the rear of the front entrance was a large assembly-classroom combination." The school had a library with a collection of reference books, maps, blackboards and desks that opened from the top. Glen Alpine Springs School was considered well-equipped for its time.

The school opened on October 22, 1902. Initially, there were fourteen day students and three boarding students; by January there were fifty-one day students and fifteen boarders. Local children attended Glen Alpine Springs Hotel, but children from as far away as South Carolina also attended. Burke County families who sent their children to the school included Bennetts, Cowans, Dales, Neills, Hennessees, Kincaids, Kirkseys and Seals. By April 1902, forty-five children were seeking enrollment as boarding students.

In order that families and students might maintain their dignity, and in order to promote industriousness, it was required that some type of payment be made for clothing provided for the children. This payment might take the form of money, work or produce provided to the school. In addition, boarders were expected to provide their own food and cook it themselves using utensils, a stove, and tables provided by the school. The boys chopped firewood to keep classrooms warm in the winter, and the girls kept the schoolroom clean.

Though initially designed as a missionary school, the curriculum at Glen Alpine Springs School included Domestic Science, Agriculture, Nature Study, Hygiene, Blacksmithing and Bible Music. The intention of the curriculum was to provide children born in a rural setting with practical coursework which would meet their needs for earning a living wage while encouraging them in their Christian faith.

In 1903, the school published a pamphlet which was distributed in hopes of garnering contributions which would make the school self-sustaining. The pamphlet was titled, "A School for Mountain Boys and Girls." The pamphlet outlined the needs of the school as well as improvements and repairs that had already taken place. It provided information on the administrative composition of the school, indicating that "a five-man advisory board for the school consisted of Frank K. Hipple, President of the Real Estate Trust Co, Philadelphia; George Wilcox of Summit, New Jersey; Edward McK. Goodwin, Superintendent of the North Carolina School for the Deaf; William Carson Ervin, a Morganton attorney; and W. Henry Grant, 156 Fifth Avenue, New York." Listed as co-principals of the school were the Reverend Mr. Schoonmaker and Mrs. Grant.

The school pamphlet also underscored the intention of its board members that the school be self-supporting while summarizing ongoing needs:

"We have raised about ten bushels of potatoes and forty-five bushels of corn. This will keep our livestock for a little time. Last year we had to buy all the oat, corn hay and fodder required to feed the two indispensable necessities—a horse and cow. Milk is at a premium and butter very scarce, grass growing only in what is called the "bottom land." We need two more teachers at an average salary of $300. Roof repaired. 17,000 shingles. One large stove for girls' kitchen. Furniture for rooms. House painted. Wagons, etc."

The silk industry, which had been a local enterprise fifty years prior to the opening of Glen Alpine Springs School, was suggested as a possible way to generate income. The Agricultural Bureau was promoting a return to the development of the silk industry, and it was debated whether or not this endeavor might prove successful. It does not appear that the school ever seriously pursued this suggestion.

Glen Alpine Springs School operated from early October through mid-May while other local public schools were open for only four months yearly. Classes were held from 9:00 a.m. to 3:00 p.m. on weekdays, and when bad weather threatened travel, day students as well as boarders stayed overnight at the school. Discipline did not appear to be a problem under the firm direction of Reverend Schoonmaker. Grades were given as numbers rather than letters, with 70 being the lowest passing grade. At the end of each academic year, the school provided an end-of-year ceremony, though not a formal graduation ceremony.

Glen Alpine Springs School operated from 1902 through 1909, at which time Reverend Schoonmaker's family encountered financial difficulties which necessitated his return to New Jersey. Though it was his intention to return to the school at some point, his leaving forced the school to close, and he was never able to reopen it. The furnishings of the Glen Alpine Springs School were sold to the Burke County Board of Education.

Fire Destroys Dilapidated Glen Alpine Springs Hotel, Famous In Past Generation

Built in 1877-78 Was Fine Building And Popular Hostelry In Its Day

INTERESTING HISTORY

When the old Glen Alpine Springs Hotel was destroyed by fire on Saturday night one of Burke county's historic buildings and a place fraught with memories for many of an older generation became an ash pile. The origin of the fire which wiped out the already dilapidated ruins of the large, rambling, 3-story frame building, is unknown, but there have been hints of incendiarism, possibly the work of marauders or the carelessness of hunters. The building was owned by Sam Goodman, of Mooresville, who owns also the tract of more than three hundred acres of mountain land surrounding. It was located south of Morganton, about 13 miles, just off of No. 181, formerly known as the old Rutherford road.

Glen Alpine Springs Hotel was built during the fall of 1877 and spring of 1878. One of the original owners and builders, John H. Pearson, oldest Morganton merchant, recalled yesterday the opening on July 17th, 1878 of what was then one of the finest hotels in Western North Carolina. Hundreds of the elite from this and adjoining states attended the banquet on that occasion and the grand opening ball. The large panelled dining hall seated two hundred people and the opening affair was a gala event.

For years before the hotel was built, even before the Civil war, the mineral springs in that locality had attracted visitors because of the fine medicinal qualities of the iron, lithia and sulphur waters. Mr. Pearson recalled that Col. Gaither, Col. Walton and oth-

(Continued on third page)

ers built cabins in that locality and during the summers their families spent some time there.

Col. T. G. Walton owned the land in the 70's when he and his son, Stanley Walton and Mr. Pearson decided to build the hotel. Donald Frazier, a Morganton merchant who had come from Scotland, had suggested to Col. Walton the picturesque name which was given to the property and which years afterwards became the name of the present town of Glen Alpine. The services of a man by the name of Collier, then residing in Morganton, a landscape gardener and architect, were employed. Mr. Pearson says that his idea had been a smaller hotel, but that once started, the enthusiasm of the architect and the other owners resulted in a large French Chateau type building, of proportions heretofore mentioned. There were 52 bedrooms in the hotel, each of a size of some modern-day apartments, none smaller than 20 ft. by 24 ft. with 18 ft. ceilings. The cost ran around $21,000, a real fortune in those days.

Walton & Pearson operated the hotel several summers successfully, attracting visitors from Charlotte, Wilmington, Columbia, New Bern and other cities downstate. An Italian band was employed and social-minded people for miles around gathered for the dances and to join with the summer sojourners in making merry at the lovely resort. At that time even the old Battery Park in Asheville had not been built.

The fame of the mineral water, as well as the social attractions, had spread abroad. It had been told that a well-known Presbyterian minister of that day Rev. "Turkey" Johnson (so called because he had served as a missionary in Turkey), had come to Glen Alpine Springs borne on a cot and the waters there had cured all his afflictions. The water was at one time shipped in large quantities to many distant points.

After the first flush of success the hotel was operated at a loss and finally was sold to a group representing the Northern Presbyterian church to be used as a school. After a time this venture, too, was abandoned and C.F. Kirksey sold the property to Clifton Pearson, son of one of the original owners, who later sold it to Mr. Goodman, who now holds the title.

References

"Bailey v. Rutjes and Others, from Burke." Synopsis of N.C. Supreme Court Decisions. The Charlotte Home and Democrat. Apr 1882.

Boggs, L.C.W. (1965). *Tales of Creekside: Historical and Supernatural*. Unpublished papers of Louise Cheesborough Walton Boggs (1899-1991).

"Eagles Nest Hotel." Carolina Mountaineer and Waynesville Courier. 25 Apr 1918.

Fick, V.G., Starnes, R.D. and Stick, D. (2006). Resorts of Western North Carolina. In *Encyclopedia of North Carolina*. University of North Carolina Press. Jan 2006.

"Fire Destroys Dilapidated Glen Alpine Springs Hotel, Famous in Past Generation." The News-Herald. 20 Nov 1936.

"Glen Alpine." Cordelia Camp's *Sketches*. The News-Herald. Progress Edition. 27 Mar 1964.

"Glen Alpine Springs." The Morning Star. 10 Sep 1886.

"Glen Alpine Springs Advertisement with Picture." The Blue Ridge Blade. 14 Sep 1878.

"Mineral Springs Hotel Was Turned Into School." The News-Herald. 19 Apr 1963.

"Morganton's 'Grand Old Man' Dies at 101." The News-Herald. 3 Jun 1954.

"Remember...." The News-Herald. 27 Aug 1984.

"Sale of Glen Alpine Springs Hotel and Lands." Unidentified newspaper. Morganton, NC. 21 Apr 1900.

"Sunrise Near Glen Alpine Springs." The Morning Star. 27 Aug 1886.

The Burke County Historical Society. (1981). *Burke County Heritage: North Carolina*. Vols. I &II, Morganton, North Carolina. Hunter Publishing: Winston-Salem, N.C.

"The Celebrated Glen Alpine Springs." The Morning Star. 29 May 1885.

"White Sulphur Springs Hotel." Carolina Mountaineer and Waynesville Courier. 4 Apr 1918.

Photographic Credits

Asheville Sulphur Springs [Hotel Belmont, postcards]. Souvenir of Asheville or the Sky-Land. Ramsey Library, UNCA. Western NC Heritage.

Eagles Nest and White Sulphur Springs, 1913. Information to Visitors Concerning Greater Western North Carolina. [Brochure]. Greater WNC Association. Inland Press: Asheville, NC.

Glen Alpine Springs, Near Morganton, Burke County, Western North Carolina. [Pamphlet]. Apr 1879.

"Haywood Springs Hotel [White Sulphur Springs Hotel, postcard]." Hunter Library Special Collections. Western Carolina University. Cullowhee, NC.

"Land of the Sky: Resorts Along the Southern Railway, Premier Carrier of the South." [Brochure] Southern Railway. Chicago, Ill.: Poole, 1915.

"Mountain Park Hotel," c.1917-1918. Adolph Thierbach. Hot Springs, NC.

"Old Spring House." Sulphur Springs Hotel. Clicks Photography. Asheville, NC.

Photographs courtesy of *Picture Burke*:
　　Colonel Thomas G. Walton.
　　　　Source: Louisa Emmons
　　Connelly Springs Hotel.
　　　　Source: Wendell Hildebrand
　　Glen Alpine Depot.
　　　　Source: R. Douglas Walker, Jr.
　　Glen Alpine Springs Hotel.
　　　　Source: R. Douglas Walker, Jr.
　　John H. Pearson. Picture Burke.
　　McEntire Inn [Hunt House] 1890.
　　　　Source: Dr. I.M Taylor.
　　Pearson Family. Picture Burke.
　　Pearson Home.
　　　　Source: Dr. I.M. Taylor
　　　　Photographer: F.W. Tyler

Thompson's Bromine Arsenic Water Springs, 1887. [Brochure]. Ashe Co, NC.

www.ingramcontent.com/pod-product-compliance
Lightning Source LLC
Chambersburg PA
CBHW081529040426

42447CB00013B/3391